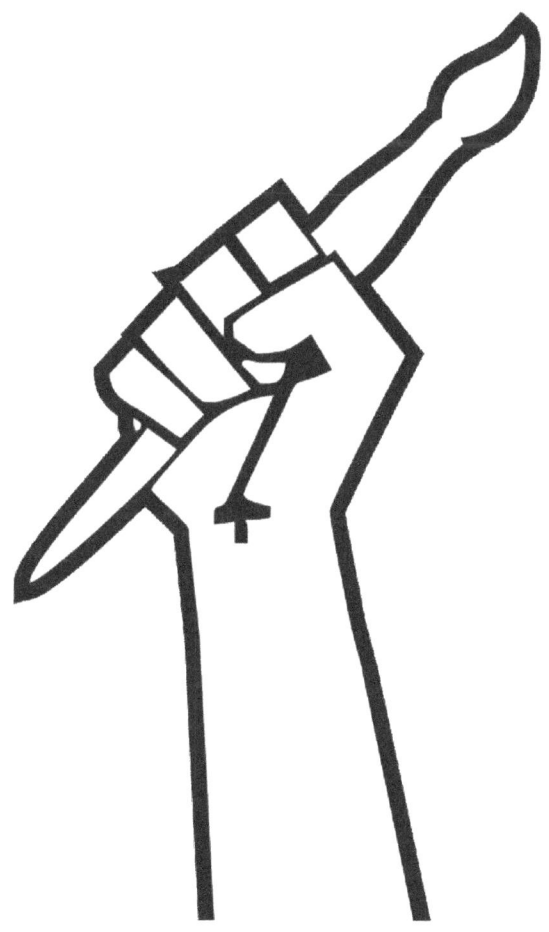

Creativity needs
ambition
without ballast.

Heinrich Denke

Content:

Leverage of your art
A adventure on the ocean of possibilities
Staying hungry
Creative rethinking

Step by step
1) Orientation
2) A short definition
3) The art market
      3.1) People on the art market
      3.2) Market Value
4) Art Marketing
5) Communication on the Market
      5.1) Content of Art
      5.2) The Public
      5.3) Communication Path
6) Sales talk

The first step
Your art is worth it,
go for it!

Make money with you art?

Yes, you can turn art into money! The good news is that this is easier to do than turning creativity into art. It is a sad truth that people who are less talented and less clever than yourself are making a lot of money with art. Right now, it is just your opinion that making money from art can be difficult. The next good news is that, by opening this book, you are already one step closer to making this happen, inasmuch as, thanks to your willingness to open this book, you have demonstrated that you possess the will to change; to go from just wanting to make money through your art to actually doing it. You have one of two qualities that are necessary to be successful on the art market, because your will to stand up for your art and to search for a solution is the most important skill that you must have. Let me congratulate you for your willingness, because, besides your willpower, all it takes is knowhow. Making money through art is the most natural, lucrative means of earning what your gift of creativity is worth. It also provides quality of life. So, the problem of making money is not really a problem in reality, because MILLIONS are made in the art market and most of this high price art isn't even good! Using the art market as leverage for our financial success is a real challenge.

Leverage of your art

The idea of this book is to open up a new point of view and way of using the art market for the leverage of your art. I have put together the experience of two decades of my work and teaching in the art market, so you can focus your energy on your art and just pick out the necessary steps, without all the trouble I went through. It is a privilege to provide you with the necessary knowledge and make it easy, fun and fast for you to stay on the path of your art career. This is because, being an artist myself, I have put much effort into building up a framework from artist to artist. My hope is that your decision to open this book will be rewarded in the form of money that you will earn and, more importantly, that you can concentrate on your art and creativity. Please follow the advice of this book, even if you are like me and have a hard time accepting and taking risks. Even by ignoring or blocking the content, this knowhow will be absorbed and open up new possibilities for you in a subconscious way, so that you can avoid going through years of struggle. This step-by-step approach that will be revealed to you soon has been proven not only by myself, but also by my students. Some of them had no artistic or business education before, and their self-esteem allowed them to draw only in secret. I cannot resist speaking out loud, stating that I am proud of them. Furthermore, when my students sold their artwork at prices that not only covered the costs of their education, but opened up a new cultural, artistic world for them, I might have felt even prouder than when I did during my big exhibitions in New York or during my first sale to a state collection. Sometimes, it is hard to believe, but you are just time period away from achieving the great results that others have achieved. All it takes is knowhow, the will to take the useful steps and the joy and experience of practice. To go down this path cheerfully knowing that it has been used throughout the centuries and will provide you with a good feeling even during the times when not everything is working out instantly. Many others like you have also been there before, and some of them, like myself, were worse off than you are, as they had no clue what to do. It was comforting for me to know, in this situation, that every artist is at the same threshold or blockade at some point in their career. We are unique in our art but our path is in a way so akin.

The framework of this book is to understand your art career as a process. It is like a sea expedition in which we have to understand how some things are occurring, to know the seas we are traveling in and why things are happening. By knowing this, we can react and adapt ourselves to the challenges to come and use them as opportunities. The ability to navigate skillfully is more useful than hoping for an autopilot solution is. After some initial experience, the knowledge will become a part of your daily art business, like a ship that becomes a captain's support, or the feeling we experience while driving our car without thinking of all the gears and mechanics that are going on in the vehicle. Get to know yourself as an artist. Know your art. Knowing the possibilities of the art market is the framework for achieving this natural feeling quickly. All we have to do is use our resources and the "winds and tides" of the art market wisely. The only way to this is to practice the navigation, find out and experience how we can use the art market so we can spend only the necessary resources and not to waste our energy that is needed to uphold our artistic outcome. This book is for helping you to get an overview and to work out what the right approach is. With time, your navigation plan will become clearer and clearer, so confusion and unexpected events will become just a disturbance on the surface. Your strong ship of artwork will deal with these waves as they clash against your ship bow.

A adventure on the ocean of
possibilities

The art market is like an expedition at sea,
and the adventure on which we have gone
will bring us back to the shores on which
things exist to support our creativity and
to leverage our art progress. Trying to
ignore and waste the possibility of art
marketing is like rowing a boat without
oars and pretending that the tide and
winds are leading us to where we want to
arrive. It is good to choose a different path,
because most artists do not make this
conscious decision. Thus, they end up in
an ocean in the middle of nowhere.
Beware; art and the art market are two
different things. Art is a part of you; a
journey that ought to grow and develop;
something that is anchored in your heart
and guts. The art market is a broad ocean
of communication and possibilities for the
artists who choose it. The art market and
marketing consist in freedom of choice;
the freedom to provide our creativity with
the best possibilities to leverage our art. It
provides those of us who are able to use a
certain knowhow with the best
environment in which we can let our art
thrive. Can art exist without the art
market? Yes, it can. And can the art
market exist without art? Sadly, it can.

With the right marketing nearly everything can be market as art. The art market is nothing less than a possibility for artists. It is up to us to use the available resources wisely and strategically, in order to take the next step in our career and make it a successes. Everything is becoming accessible. The keys to success are our willpower and knowledge. What you are reading right now contains the main points to gain the knowledge that you need. The best part is that the necessary knowledge lies within the few pages that are before you. You have already taken the first and most difficult step – that is, summoning your willpower and making your choices. Free yourself from the propaganda according to which any change in the art market is feared and artists are fearful to make the decision to act on their own. This freedom of mind will open your potential and energy, as well as allow you to invest in what is beneficial for your art. Starting from when I am writing these lines, that will be available to you soon, you have the same chances of being successful as an established gallery does. You are even better off than established art galleries, because you are not burdened by old habits that do not work and are only any good at stifling new possibilities.
Art is always a chance to change the point of view of what we take for grounded and to take a position to be thankful for every

opportunity. There are some rare moments in life when this thankfulness is very present. As I was teaching classical statue drawing in Louvre to a young student from Iran, marked by the troubled upcoming of his region of origin, it occurred to me how simple, easy and fun culture can transfer value to everyone's life. By that, I do not mean the great classical art practice approaches like from Charles Bargue that I was teaching, but the pleasure that he had in showing me how our art has roots going back to the Persian culture. Who also could imagine that the same student with his "cultural disadvantages" would turn out to be one of the best in adopting the classical western drawing approach. Another of my students (who started without any desire to approach the art market), told that, by being successful and earning money through her artwork, she started feeling like a real artist and it opened up potential in her. The will is in most of the cases more important than the starting point or believe. Yes, it is possible to work as an artist without touching the art market, but there is a deep need of contribution in us as artists and the need to balance our creative outcome with wealth so that our art may thrive in the best possible way.

Staying hungry

If you still thinking that your starting
position could be better and you still feel
uncertain about your current situation,
then let me tell you about the advantage of
this disadvantage. Art history and
experience have proven that, if an artist is
starting out from a struggling position,
they can keep up the feeling of "ambition"
and draw his or her power from the feeling
of having deserved what was out of reach
before. I myself came from a struggling
position in which confusion was created by
post-war Europe and the fact that I did
not belong to the cultural freedom of the
west. This was the best starting point for
me and my success proofed it. My parents
risked everything, absolutely everything, in
order to give me the possibility to thrive in
a cultural environment. If my father had
been summoned during the escape from
Schlesia (which was part of East Germany
after the war under the Soviet Polish
occupation, and is now thankfully reunited
with the rest of Europe), my father would
have been shoot. My parents had to give
up everything, like the company my father
had founded, to obtain false visas to flee to
Germany. Once in the West, our family
had to start from scratch again. But the
craving for freedom and culture was
making us hungry enough to get the

necessary knowledge to rebuild our lives. The fact that I went through school as an outsider, or that I decided to study art as a soldier in the middle of the post communistic wars, is my proof that hunger for culture will always find a way to make things work. So, success is based on keeping up this hunger. Even after my art studies, which, like on automatic pilot, were leading me to be broke, there was always a voice inside me telling that the next book, the next piece of information, would shine, forming a path out of the darkness. Let me tell you that, if you believe that academic art study guarantees an art career, you are mistaken. Every artist has a story of struggle to tell; the idea that some ready-made path exists for academic artists is simply false. Perhaps that is why so many people love artist biographies: where there is art, there is an essential struggle and such a good story to be told. For myself, this hunger and light leading me forward never died out. They are alive to this day. Even after my New York exhibition, I was certain that the next challenge was just around the corner. An old, wise artist once told me: "Only effortless success is the certain defeat of an artist and his art". Your story of struggle is an essential part of your story as an artist. Remember reading the chapters, that behind the knowledge there is a real sorry of my struggle or a struggle of a artist I helped, until the solution or this framework you read was figured out. My struggle paid off and caused me to want to create the lines that you are reading, so that you can pick your battles more wisely. After going through all of those years of struggle, I made a vow to myself: the vow to do my best, so that every other artist could concentrate more on their gift of creativity. If I had known the system that will be revealed to you in some pages a decade ago, I would have paid any price for that knowledge. You are living at a good time for artists to start out on the art market. Your decision, willpower and the knowhow that you are going to learn can easily provide you with money from your art, and they will prevent you from losing precious time.

Creative rethinking

A lot has changed since the times when the living of an artist depended on the art market and was a challenge and a problem. We are living in a time of choices. These choices no longer depend on the art market mechanism that led our ancestors to despair. Our time is one of the best times for artists; we can choose to ignore the art market and survive, OR we can choose to use it to our advantage and thrive. At a time when everybody can reach

out and communicate with everybody, we
have become equal to those who once
controlled everything in the art market. It
has taken some time to establish the new
means of communication and open some
minds to the new systems and
possibilities, so the best time to take
control of your art career is right now!
The only think that you need is to trust
this YES from the very beginning. You
have nothing to lose, and your art has
much to gain. The safe way to earn what
your art deserves is to to keep reading, to
take in the necessary knowledge, to keep
up your willpower. Will it be easy? Yes,
because, as an artist, you have a big
advantage on the art market. Just think of
those who, unlike you, do not have the
integrity or the gift of an artist, and who
are still making a lot of money with the art
of others. Imagine what you could do, with
the advantage of having the knowledge,
being an insider and sitting at the source
of what other art dealers are in desperate
need to do in order to take part in the art
market.
An art collector once told me : "No matter
how much you will earn with your art,
nothing will make you feel as rich as the
possession of creativity does." Start feeling
rich right away, thanks to your creativity.
This vibe will soon draw the people who
will depend on you to you. They depend
on something that they cannot acquire,

and pay money for it. They pay for the fetish of what they cannot create themselves - your artwork. This direct connection between creativity and culture is precious and will soon pay off.

Many artists fear becoming a businessman or losing touch with the artistic side of things, because of the art market. This depends of the company you pick. It was a big problem until I was lucky enough to discover techniques that build on the artists' strengths, like cultural and personal empathy which you will learn about in the "Art Talk" chapter. Becoming a sales person would be a big disadvantage to you, authenticity is a big advantage nowadays. Buying art directly from a real artist is an important criterion. Selling art can be your source of communication about your art and for new ideas. Soon, it will become an important part of your art, as will taking a fresh look at your art and being able to see your art through the eyes of others. It is a possibility to expand your view, but without losing your closeness to your art or authenticity. The step to "sell off as artist" would make you just another art dealer, so hold on to your individuality. By reading this chapter entirely, you have already proven that you have made the necessary decision and possess the necessary willpower to succeed. You can use this potential to transform your will

into success and to open your creativity up
to a new world of freedom and wealth.

Step by step

As unique and individual as you are, and as individual as your art is, it is important that your approach to the art market is just as individual. The main concept of this book is not to provide a formula to follow blindly, but to give your creativity the chance to develop via clear knowledge of your individual path.

1) Orientation

Artists are often reluctant to even consider producing their work in a commercial sense. Instead, they privately sell or give their works away as presents to friends and relatives. However, strictly speaking, forms of business relationships often begin with this transmission of works of art – this is a very early and simple stage, but one which is already part of the art market: the minute an object changes hands, commercial activity is occurring. Some people like to argue that money is not everything. This is really only too true, as the art market does not restrict itself to letting goods flow back and forth in exchange for money. The art market is more – and people often forget about this: public attention, fame, reputation, names which artists make for themselves, all of this is created from the interaction between the different participants in the market activity.

An art work's market value and quality are all too often two completely different things, because, unfortunately, the situation has developed in such a way that not everything is successful on the market. Even good art is often not to the market's taste. Who does not know what happened to the impressionists, who were labelled as amateurs and derided by their contemporaries? Decades later, their work fetches the highest price time and time again. The art which rubs the current market up the wrong way could impact the future in a significant manner, because really influential ideas, which survive over time, come from the non conformists, who take bold steps and create something new, rather than comfortably repeat something which is familiar.

2) A short definition

Most of artist have a strange fear of economic terms. The good news is that for our art career we can avoid the most and break it down to the view necessary.

Marketing is one of the crucial functions of economic activity. The purpose of these concepts is to bring a product to the man or to the woman – to bring it to the customers. In economic terms, the term *Market* designates the meeting of the offer of a good and of the demand for that good.

It works in accordance with the basic principle of exchange : an offer of something is made, in exchange of a medium of exchange

3) The art market

The participants in the art market come from various spheres, pursue different objectives and have certain expectations ; however, this connects their interest in art. The expression of the value is in the economic sense of the term - mostly money. The more market participants are involved in an art sale, the more the art increases in value.

3.1) People on the art market

The participators to the art market are, on the one hand, of course, artists , who fabricate the "goods" in the first place, as art producers and art sellers. The art buyers , who may be representatives of the private sector or of the public sector, encounter them. Municipalities and public museums buy art, but so do companies and private persons, who collect paintings, for example. They all link the interest in art and the joint interaction in the market, with the objective of making a profit. This allows the artist sell his work in exchange of money, while the buyer acquires an appreciation of his assets against payment. Furthermore, there is a third group of participants which takes part in this complex trade relation. It is the group of Art intermediaries. This group has become necessary, due to the art market's complexity. Agencies, galleries, and trade fair organisations simplify the selling and the purchasing of art, the transfer of art between artists and people who are interested in art, and are often establish the art market in the first place. They make their profit from the improvement of communications and transactions between buyer and seller. In this relationship network, opinions about art and artists get built. These opinions reciprocally influence each-other or put each-other into perspective. For example, reviews of a young artist's exhibition, which are published in a trade journal, can give the artist a public reputation, which can arouse the interest of potential buyers. Conversely, if an artist is slated in a publication, this can cause damage to an artist's prominence. The latter case of affairs, in particular, can also be used positively, in order to increase the artist's popularity – that is, if clever marketing is applied.

It is for this reason that the opinions which have been formed about an artist in the art market are of the utmost importance for the artist's market position. It is essential to share in the formation of opinions within an art network, and to maintain contact with as many renowned and experienced market participants who have authority over the formation of opinions, as possible. What it means to successfully join forces with a certain network of experts, which by no means is "chumming up" with contacts, will be discussed more precisely later on.

The structure of a network is all the more important , because the group of artists who market themselves within the market is very large, and the self-marketing artists have little influence on the market situation: there are far more offers for works of art than there customers for works of art. Despite this, there is an oversupply of "commodity art", which successfully manages to take part in the art market. Finding the right cooperation partners plays a decisive role in success. Within the market hierarchies, this situation is referred to as Starter Market. In this starter market, a great deal of art sellers want to sell their works to few buyers: the offer exceeds the demand.

In contrast, the situation of the Secondary Market is reversed. Should an artist establish himself in the first place, and should his works of art reach high prices, there would be a high demand, which would largely exceed the limited demand. These processes can be compared to the stock market processes: even in the stock markets, there are secure shares – the so-called "Blue Chips" - which are very popular. The demand exceeds the offer, thus it pushes up the market value's prices. We will deal with capital investments in art in more detail later on. These two examples present extreme situations; in-between these extremes, there are numerous nuances of the market development. The particular characteristics of the various markets will be once again addressed in detail later on. However, to begin with, we must deal with what value means in the art market.

3.2) Market Value

It's important to understand that in the art market we are dealing with value in the economic sense of the term. It's a matter of evaluating a producer and his products with regard to his chances of participating in the market's sales activities and reaching high exchange value. It is important for the seller to earn money, while the buyer searches for valuable investment opportunities. What is meant by this is not the prime importance of the ideal and intrinsic value of art, although this does play an important role in the very weighty creation of an opinion in the art market. It is important for artists to have a clear understanding that the artistic quality of their works is not the (only) decisive factor, and that an assessment of their individual market chances is not only based on this.

The construction of this added value constitutes the foundation which consists of the qualities, or the requirements of artists. These requirements can be broken down into three parts: the artist himself, the type of his art and his position in the market. These three principles form the artist's initial situation in the market and they decide on the added market value which can be created while the artist's career is being built.

art market potentials

The potential of a artist in the art market can be imagine as a barrel model. No matter how high some of the planks in the side of the barrel are, the shortest one will decide how high the water can be filled in. If you imagine the potential of a art career as the water, it's understandable to maintain all planks as high as possible. In order to do this, it is important to increase the individual planks of the barrel, because a barrel can only be filled up to the lowest bar. When applied to our model, this means that the total value of a certain sector can only be as good as its worst condition. Few resources are available in a barrel. Hence, work must be done on it, in order to make up for and to compensate for this deficit as well as possible. The artist must research his weakness and work on for example coping with stressful situations better. Similarly, a painter could refine his creative techniques even more, by experimenting with other materials, or by implementing new techniques. There are numerous possibilities, which can be selected in the individual situations. This would be the barrel model that define the strength and weaknesses as a artist in the art market. During the art career 2 more "barrels" are geting important. With the sections "artist", the "art", and "market" also has a influence on the art career. The aim is to fill the capacities of all three containers as much as possible. Even the third barrel, named "market", can be optimised in this sense, by means of skilful marketing. In these cases,   professional support from somebody who is experienced is an asset in the long run.

The artist himself as a foundation of the added market value

In the art market, it is acceptable to draw lots of attention to yourself. Young artists are expected to be present at exhibitions or at art fairs. Everybody buys "art experience". In turn, this requires artists to have strong personalities, so that they can cope with these market requirements, which are often associated with stress. The willingness to approach people and to be able to be convincing during direct contact with people plays an important role. Furthermore, there is the question about the career of a meaningful artist. Did he study in an art school, or is he a "lateral entrant" who has developed his skills himself. Even in this respect, lots of artists make certain claims about their desired "goods". Some galleries only take on artists who have an academic background under contract.

In order to clarify the different demands and interests which buyers on the art market have, two examples of artists and their respective target groups , as well as the market mechanisms , should be presented at this stage. It is obvious that this consists in a schematization, in which there might, understandably, be overlaps and intermediate stages. The crucial distinctive features represent the artist's self image , therefore the manner in which the artist generates the content of his art and how he sees himself in a broader context.

Most likely in the beginning of his carrier the works of an artist, whose art is a reflection of his inner self, are an expression of his experience of the world. His position in the art market is determined on the basis of this self-expression. Buyers are admirers and lovers of this art, which appeals to their taste.

Later the artist is involving more influence in his work. An artist's work does not only reflect his personal experience of the world, but it also is a comment on events in general. It fills internal and external requirements. His works reflect the spirit of the times and are bought as records of our culture, as well as documents of the spirit of our times. This example points out that an artist's perception of himself can catch the fancy of two different kinds of buyers. One type of buyer is more interested in the personality cult, whereas the other is more interested in obtaining documentation of our time via the medium of art. This is broadening the group of his art buyers.

If we go back to think the artist as a factor of successes in the "barrel" model, the art history has proven that artist with certain values are more successful, like outstanding:

- Artistic personality
- Social network
- Personal development
- art concept
- Financial security
- Art training
- Recognition in the work
- Continuity of career

The genre of art as the foundation of the market value

Let us return to our initial question, which was about the basics of the market value's structure. In addition to the person of the artist, the type of art which the artist produces consists in a significant evaluation criterion for the potential participant in the market. This includes the ideal value of the works, their force of expression from a point of view of art history and even the statement which is expressed in the works of art. This is opening a broader view though the art: do the works criticize society, are they a comment on the spirit of the times, are they part of a comprehensive art theory, or else are they intuitive, emotional statements?

The seemingly simple , yet very significant physical characteristics of the works must not be neglected. Is it a painting, a sculpture or video art? Is the material durable, in good conditions, very big, very small, and can it be transported without any major effort? Art buyers are reluctant to invest in objects, if there is a risk that decay of the object's material could cause the object to decrease in value shortly after it has been bought. Lots of photographic works, which are really cheap from a material point of view, sometimes increase in value, for instance, by being transferred on large silver paper by means of an elaborate projection technique. The type of art and the elaboration are influencing the value in the market.

If we go back to think the genre of art in the "barrel" model, possible factors for successes could be outstanding value in:

- Individual art technique
- Philosophical content
- Zeitgeist / social commentary
- Spirituality
- Psychology of Perception
- Art Historical classification
- Unique feature
- Transportability
- Continuity of the type
- Condition
- Technical execution

The art market's situation as a foundation of the market value

In addition to the factors which make up an artist and his works marketability and market value, is a third factor, which determines the evaluation of an art producer in a decisive manner. This third factor is the market itself. What are the market circumstances, what art trends are loved? Questions such as if an artist is ready to be represented in the market, if he or she has built a network, if he or she has already reached a certain level of popularity, and, if so, in what areas and what particular art galleries and agencies are relevant, determine what development work must be accomplished. A lot more marketing efforts need to be carried out for a new comer than for an artist who is already well known. At this point, the merchandising features of art are brought up again – is art satisfying current taste? Is it "new", market fresh, or is it based on something which has already been done before?

If we go back to think the given art market in the "barrel" model, some criteria for a market approach would be helpful:
- Market conditions
- Market taste
- Presence in the market
- Market network
- Price trend
- Provenance
- Novelty on the market
- Market continuity
- Liquidity

3.3) Types of art markets

The conditions of an artist in the art
market, which were discussed in the
previous chapter, also give him access to
different markets. The designations for the
different types of market have already
been discussed, although we have not
clarified them.
All artist begin as a newcomer to the art
market. In these starter market the selling
of art take place by the artist selling
directly to the customer. This market is
the springboard market for many artists
who have to market themselves in the
beginning. Later on the artist is moving to
the primary market. In the primary
market, on the other hand, trade is done
via an intermediary. As a general rule, this
intermediary is a gallery. In the meantime,
the artist has succeeded at finding his
first professional art representation, which
makes a much larger segment of the
market accessible to him. The art career
moves later on to the secondary market.
On the secondary market, the sale via
more intermediary positions is organized,
e.g. galleries, agencies, exhibitions, auction
houses. These transactions by the
participants in the market also requires
time-consuming communication, and high
potential of the market value. The more
market participants are involved in an art
sale, the more the art increases in value .

The long term goal for a successful market participation, therefore, is to build up a position on the secondary market.

3.4) A Career as an Artist

With the knowledge of the afore-mentioned factors, which influence an art producer's performance and his product on the market, an artist can trace the course of his career. Important steps of a "career path in the market" can be observed in the majority of cases. Understanding the own career as a process is important, it makes possible to define the position of our own situation in the market. By this means, the appropriate, promising marketing operations can be specifically chosen.

In simple terms, an artist's Market Career comprises five stages. In the beginning, there is the person who is interested in art: this person initially deals with art out of personal interest. They decide to deepen their interest by signing up for art studies or by self-educating themselves further. About 70 percent of people who are interested in art choose to do this. Only about 20 percent of beginners remain by the end of the training period. These people gain their market experience, then they try and lay the foundation for their career on the starter market. In turn, barely 10 percent of these newcomers to the art market successfully break even after a few years, and gradually penetrate the primary market, by cooperating with other participants in the market (galleries etc.). Mechanisms prevail within this market. These mechanisms make it possible to make high profits by selling art. On the other hand, however, they intensify the selectivity amongst art producers. Only about 0,01 percent of artists can establish themselves in the secondary market and fetch the best prices.

As already discussed, an artist's sales success depends largely on his market value. For a newcomer to the starter market, who is not very widely known, competition is high: the offer of art is high; however, the demand for art is low. The risk of loss is considerably high for art buyers in this situation, as artists might unexpectedly change their style, abandon their careers and say goodbye to the art world. Thus, a started collection would be worthless. Therefore, the starter market is made up predominantly of potential buyers; amongst them are art lovers who buy things which are to their personal taste . There are fewer collectors in this market. Collectors buy art as an investment, which they can re-sell for a profit at a later date. From this point of view, one could talk of the potential which art buyers have to increase or to reduce an artist's career in the market.

The progress of an artist's career is characterized by different potentials, which determine an artist's market value, much like finance and the market position do. Let us focus on the different phases of an artist's career once again and observe the course of the potential within the individual phases from this point of view. The Risk Potential describes the situation to which the art buyers commit themselves by purchasing a work of art. As expected, this risk is particularly high for young artists, who are newly represented on the art market. The more established and renowned an artist has become, the lower the danger in capital investment is for the buyer.

Along with the risk of early investment, is the chance that the works of an artist will gain market value. Whoever has acquired inexpensive works can sell them lucratively, should a career boost occur. This Profit Potential is the highest in the case of artists whose works have not been on the market for too long, but who have obtained a certain status and who are beginning to establish themselves on the primary market. The Liquidity of Works, i. e. the possibility to resell them profitably, increases for popular artists.

As already described, the risk potential is very high for newcomers to the market. The risk only subsides slowly, in the transition to the primary market. This is because the likelihood that an artist will keep to his chosen path goes up.   Even the possibility for an artist to establish themselves on the art market, coupled with the greater demand for their works, causes the profit potential to go up, and the artist's career to get a boost. I see the rise of the frequent link between art and profit potential as problematic. Now, the artist is becoming interesting for market scouts as well, because market scouts try to increase their profit by targeting the promotion of newly discovered art talents. Incidentally, market scouts do not play a significant role as gatekeepers – that is, as decisive opinion-makers - at the intersections of segments of the art market, because they leverage the artists to a certain market presence. With the growth of the recognition of an artist's name, and the increasing demand for an artist's work, the liquidity of the works by a renowned artist becomes easier to re-sell. This market integration enables the transition into the primary market.

In this market sector, two phases can be distinguished: during the initial establishment of the artist, the capital investment risk subsides, whereas the demand grows. Therefore, the profit potential increases, and the artist becomes more interesting for short-term investors, who are hoping for a short term or medium term increase in value. The more this market status hardens, the more the risk potential subsides, while, at the same time, the liquidity of an artist's art works steadily increases. After an artist has been present on the market for longer, however, prices become stable. Therefore, the accumulation of value becomes clearer; however, it is no longer possible to make any high profit margins by the means of an unexpected increase in value. The profit potential slowly drops.

In this situation, the artist can reach the secondary market. The course of his career becomes clearer, while the development of his art and his position in the art market become more predictable. The artist becomes interesting in the eyes of long-term investors, collectors, museums and major investors. Publications, auctions and exhibitions ensure further renown and increase in value. However, the prices of the artist's works are correspondingly high, they are no longer so easy to sell and the liquidity curve slowly drops. Basically, the only possible buyers are art collectors and museums, which can afford to pay large sums of money to store an object of such high value. The artist and his works become a secure attribute for value retention. Again, something similar can be observed, such as at the interface between the starter market and the primary market: long-term investors use similar mechanisms to the ones which art scouts use. They acquire established works of art, which they consider to be a safe investment option, and, with this investment, they see to it, that these works reach a certain rank (the rank of valuable art) and that they stay in that rank.

The development of a market presence in the different types of market can also be organised according to geographical preferences. Being renown on the market stretches from a starter market which is primarily regionally oriented (the artist tries to sell his art in his immediate surroundings) through to the primary market on a national level (the gallery owner or the agency tries to introduce the artist in other cities as well), to an international secondary market (the artist does business between art galleries at international trade fairs). This gradation is indeed the most desirable development of an artist's market presence, as numerous possibilities can arise from it. The highly traded secondary market takes place on a regional and on a national level. Conversely, international customers also buy from galleries that act as intermediaries between artists and customers (primary market). Likewise, an international starter market is possible. In this market, artists and customers would have direct contact , e.g. by means of the internet.

3.5) *Places to sell art*

Before we can take a look at the crucial questions concerning the structure of a market presence, there is yet another important aspect regarding the art market segments which needs to be examined. The afore-mentioned developments of an artist's career on the art market can also be traced in the ambit of distribution facilities , that is, the places in which art is "distributed", or offered for sale. In accordance with the different types of customers which exist in the market segments, distribution facilities (Points of Sale) develop. They cater to different purchase demands.

For the artists who are still unknown, the starter market takes place predominantly in private settings (***Private Trade).*** Self-organised exhibitions in the artists' own quarters or in the offices of acquaintances give them the opportunity to win over art lovers with their work. Even the possibilities for presentation and for sale, which are available by means of the internet, should not be neglected, as they open up the possibility of extending the boundaries of the frame of reference to a national and an international level from this early stage onwards.

More sales opportunities in a private setting would include selling to friends and relatives , street sales , private presentations , exhibitions in offices , sales during special events , studio openings, art clubs in their own city .

Artists have succeeded at establishing themselves in these small settings. Groups of artists, art clubs and/or public establishments often offer opportunities for exhibitions for artists who are newcomers. This creates the opportunity to expand the area of interest on to regional and national level. A wider public, in which art gets a great deal of attention, develops. In bigger exhibitions, art galleries can be attentive and offer contracts. Thus, **_Low Trade_** employs intermediaries to interact with the art market. Thus, artists get the opportunity to build links with art market participants who are already established (art galleries, etc.) and that occupy a higher ranking position. In this sense, artists can benefit from their market value. The following are other possible sales and presentation locations: a great selection of galleries , public facilities , exhibitions / facilities in buildings , smaller auction houses and smaller art fairs.

In the best case scenario, and particularly by supporting galleries with skilful marketing strategies and individual promotional activities , artists eventually achieve the status which has already been discussed in detail. This status is the status of a participant in the international secondary art market, which is called *„**High Trade**"* in the (art) metropolis of the world. An artist in that position would be represented in major art fairs, famous auction houses, renowned art collections, and, finally, museums of contemporary art would invest in their works.

The crucial question for an artist who wants to build up a position in the market is based on the following queries mainly: How do I get a market presence? How do I establish contact with appropriate partners in the art market, who can help me in my current development stage? How do I establish added market value which will make me interesting in the eyes of these established participants in the market, so that I can benefit from their higher-ranking position in the art market? Despite their complexity, the artist can handle these questions. What is important is the selection of useful measures which exist within the market; the market tools. In the next chapter, we will discuss what these market tools are and how you apply them.

4) Art Marketing

After we have dealt with the structures and workings of the art market, we can focus on the more specific questions, like how a successful participation in the market can be built. This is where the task of the art marketing comes in. Successful arts marketing is based on certain techniques, on the market tools and on a strategy for applying those tools. The better these means of aid are handled, the easier and more certain it is for an artist to assert themselves on the art market.

In order to establish a position for yourself on the art market, the artist need various aids. These **Market Tools** include **Know-how, Publishing, Networking** and **Presenting**. The interaction of these four basic marketing skills opens up excellent opportunities to exist on the art market, as they help to create added market value. Incidentally, they must not be limited to one person only, often this is not even possible, given the art market's requirements. By collaborating with several people who each bring their own particular skills to the table, you can create a fertile and successful marketing concept.

Know-how:

Know-how means in-depth knowledge of the art market and its mechanisms; likewise, knowledge of art in its numerous facets is essential. *This even includes information about historical, political and social events.*

Publishing:

In order to build a reputation as a serious and "valuable" artist who can survive in the art market, it is highly important to create public reviews. Professional publications, such as monographs and catalogues, as well as articles in art magazines, press and television can create a basis for a level of awareness that reaches both scientific circles and laymen art.

Networking:

The structure of the broadest possible network of experts helps to share experiences, to obtain information and specific knowledge. Few things are as valuable as personal acquaintances with other market participants, be they collector circles or potential buyers, be they scientific, specialist circles, journalists or arts organizations. They all help to establish and strengthen an artist's market position. Finally, the "word of mouth" factor, which is the personal disclosure of information and recommendations, is not to be underestimated when it comes to developing a reputation in the art market. This subheading also indicates how to benefit from the contacts in your networks, such as galleries, art agencies, art Consultants, which act as "multipliers".

Presenting:
 Of course, presenting works of art consists in one of the most important elements for developing the artists market position. Participating in exhibitions and in art fairs attracts attention. This is one of the most important interfaces for presenting art, however, it is also important to take part in art tenders and competitions, as this can play an important role in the path to conquering a successful market position.

Sensible use of these market tools could be made in order to develop an artist's career. It is important for a newcomer to the " starter market " to appear in public and to exhibit their work at least once. Group exhibitions are offered for this purpose. This allows contacts to be established, and first experiences with the selection and the organisation of artists' own works of art to be collected in the context of an exhibition . In general, comments on exhibitions are made in the media, and individual names become well-known. In the ambit of the primary market, if an artist already has a degree of public notoriety, collects his first market experiences and establishes contacts, his market position should be extended. Individual group exhibitions, and additional group exhibitions in big cities and on a national level provide even more publicity. Reports in the national press and on television are helpful. What was said before about a solid contact network is also valid here: if the contact network is constantly expanded, the chances of successfully participating in the market go up significantly.

If the artist has attained a position on the international secondary market, he can build this position up even more by the means of scientific publications, articles in professional magazines, art symposiums, and by building contacts in international art fairs. The sensible use of certain market tools within the market segments is aimed primarily at maximising financial profit. Yet, it must not be forgotten that, in order to maximise financial profit, you also need the other added market values , as they are closely interrelated and they build on each other, or they often form a prerequisite.

In order to be able to use market tools in a useful manner, it is often appropriate to provide the necessary conditions for their optimal use beforehand. For an artist who is in need of a reputation in the market, it is important for the artist to attract the attention of other participants in the art market, for example, by the means of time-consuming efforts or publications.

Thereby, additional possibilities open up , such as exhibitions, which help to make a reputation grow even more.

However, this can only ever be achieved by the means of exchange with other market participants. A gallery that causes people to talk about it a lot, due to organising spectacular exhibitions, has a corresponding reputation in the art scene at its disposal. This opens up even more possibilities for the gallery in question to participate in the art market. The gallery can charge higher prices for its art. In order for an artist to be able to benefit from this art gallery's market position, the artist must consider what they can offer the gallery, so that the gallery can then build on the artist's market position even more. How would the gallery benefit from collaborating with the artist? Does the artist innovative art make for an extravagant exhibition, which has never taken place before? Will the press pay any attention to the gallery as well, because of these works? Will the fancy of the gallery's regular customers be taken, or will a whole new market be attracted to my works in the gallery? The answer to qustion like this is opening the exchange with other market participants for a win-win situation.

5) Communication on the Market

Now that we have familiarized ourselves with the nature and the key functions of the art market, we can focus on the question of how we can successfully participate in the market itself.
Art always involves communication. We will talk about the content of art, about the artist and about his works. It is therefore important for artists to be clear on the following questions: What does my art want; what does it expresses (**content of my art**)? Who do I affect with my works, who is interested in them (**audience**)? And finally: How can I carry out exchanges with the interested parties (**marketing strategy**)?
Learning about these three main themes helps artists to determine their own positions, and it creates an ideal starting point from which to successfully participate in the art market.

5.1) Content of Art

First of all, we want to spend time on the content of our art. Many artists make the mistake of offering a whole "vendor's tray" of creative possibilities; on the one hand, they are putting their ingenuity to the test;

on the other hand, they are also hoping that they will score by offering an abundance of works. Although, for building an art career, it makes sense to use your own resources to "get to the heart of something", rather than to scatter yourself thinly all over the place. Even artists who create their works emotionally, from the gut , are acutely aware that there are certain common features that distinguish their pictures. We must have a clear idea of our artistic identity while taking the path to successfully participating in the art market. Only then can we create a characteristic " brand" that we offer to the public. This economic language sounds more daunting than it actually is: it is simply a matter of being aware of your own position and of finding out which special features distinguish your own work. Because this is precisely what makes your own art valuable; what arouses interest and causes your works to differ from other artists' works. This is also true for artists who are already aware of their own position; it is not an error to be aware of and to understand the following steps. The first step in the development of your own art identity consists in analysing your inventory ,in a manner which is similar to the previously discussed three areas of the barrel models (see chapter 3). Assessing your starting point is not easy at first. For example, you have to self-

examine yourself subjectively and draw
conclusions about the market participants
or about the public from an objective point
of view. However, it is crucial that, from as
early as possible, you bear in mind
whether or not the qualities which you
possess, and of which you are confident,
are understood as such by outsiders.
One of the first important steps in the
clarification of your position consists in a
concise collection of the works which you
have done until now. Should there be no
catalogue of works, it is a good idea to
create one. By confronting yourself and
your past, certain factors emerge and
become apparent. They keep on appearing,
and they play a particular role in your
work. By comparing personal life
experience with the development of artistic
creation, it is possible to define a main
objective. Although this requires some
time, it is the only way to succeed in
finding the central theme in your work:
what do my art works express, what
makes them special and differentiates
them from other works of art?
If you have recognised the essential ideas
of your works, you can classify the works
which you have done until present from
this point of view. This will be the next
step for you. Different working methods
and perspectives on your own work
become clear. During this step,
outstanding series of works can be made

available to people who would be interested in them, for example in the form of a catalogue. By working on the substantive basis of your own artistic creations, you can gain a view of your future works.: under what point of view have I not yet elaborated this essential issue, and how can I get to the heart of it better? The works, in which the very core of your creations is expressed so clearly, can be presented in a public exhibition (retrospective). Hence, it is possible to observe if my artistic creations and the central issues of my art are understandable for and accessible to the public. It is important for the observer to understand the works without ant (significant) additional explanations.

5.2) The Public

" The best art benefits no-one if it is just piled up in the basement." This sentence gets right to the heart of an artist's situation. Art needs an observer, because it is a means of communication. It creates a dialogue between the person who creates it and the people who are interested in it. However, this encounter must be brought on its way first – and that is not so easy to do nowadays. Artists invest a lot of energy in their works; however, they are then disappointed when they see that contents do not convey themselves. The exchange between artists and their audience must be developed step by step. If the observer is considered to be part of the art process, then a successful form of communication in the art market is much more likely to take place. But even when the public already exists, the perspectives and the claims of artistic creation can be expressed even more clearly.

Therefore, artists should deal with the following question starting from early on: who is interested in my art? In simple terms, it is possible to distinguish people who might be interested in our art in two respects: firstly, you can distinguish individuals and figure out their personal taste; secondly, you can distinguish their societal role. Both criteria influence the observer's interests. At this point, the remarks by different types of art buyers should be remembered. According to these remarks, art buyers either buy art which satisfies their personal taste, or they buy art as a financial investment. In a later chapter we will get to the core of the buyer motivation.

Firstly, let us focus on the taste, which is not open to dispute. There are different models for contemplating and for evaluating taste. A triangle model is easy to imagine and has been tried and tested for the evaluation of taste in art. This model can classifies taste as field between 3 main taste characteristics. Depending on art and market the main poles can be define different. A good suggestion for the art market of the point between the three following poles could be: „Balance", whose attributes are between pleasure and discipline, "stimulant", whose properties vary between fantasy and adventure, and "dominance", whose demands lie between Thrill and control. It is important to study the group that is already interested or is buying the art of a artist, to research which dominant criteria of art taste they could be contained in.

Behind these seemingly abstract property zones, concrete , conceivable groups of people with their taste tendencies are hiding: the conservatives hold the „Balance" between pleasure and control. Concepts such as nostalgia, family, security, tradition and quality are typical factors which appeal to this public. In this way we can define main target groups for our art.

Similarly, the impression which you have of your own works, as regards to taste, can be classified into the tendency triangle. Although art is always complex and ambiguous, whether a work of art seems more nostalgic or rebellious, can mostly be determined. There is a correlation between your own works and a group of interested people , so it can be assumed that these works are suitable for this audience. In addition to the intended content or characteristics of the art, the representations of the works are taken into account. The content of a work of art and the manner in which the work of art is represented should be consistent, in order to make it easier for the observer to access the relevant topic. Let us consider the example of a work of art with contents lightness and esprit, but which has a colour scheme which is full of contrasts and is designed in an aggressive manner. In this case, the visual impression and substantive issues would not comply with each-other. Therefore, the painting would not appeal to those who are interested in the really essential content of lightness. It may be that, out of your preferred qualities, the liberal, arduous ones, or the ones which need an explanation, will access art. Publicity for this kind of art would probably miss its target audience.

After we have considered the correlation between art content and the public's taste, we will focus on an additional characteristic of our potential buyers. The social role profile of those who are interested in art mirrors the social characteristics of the people who we sought out in the taste profile, earlier on. This public role profile describes the social "lavel" in which the interested people are to be found most frequently. For instance, landscape representations are far more likely to appeal to a middle aged buyer than to teenagers.

 The observations about the social characteristics of our buyers help to clear up important questions. The three basic social characteristics of age, gender and social status can clarify numerous questions concerning how contacts are built . Let us consider the example of an art which conveys the search for your inner self, for Balance and something heavenly. These contents attract the interest of people whose lives are determined by emotions which are similar to the ones that they confirm that they see in art. Now, we must get to the bottom of what the age, gender and status of the people who we draw close to our target group is, and what problems they tackle most of all. It is rarely possible to determine an exclusive target group: however, by doing so, we are drawing closer to some potential addressees at whom we can aim the communication concept for acquiring our art. These initial assumptions should be substantiated through discussion and research. Often, individual purposes in life and individual situations can be gathered from a possible audience. Such observations are best engaged in conversation with friends and acquaintances, but also with neutral experts of the art market. The end result is the clearest possible picture in which people who are interested in the topic of art, and who understand and appreciate it, are to be found.

 Incidentally, there are also artists who take an unconventional path and want to irritate specific groups of people by means of offensive themes, which is to say that they address the wrong groups with their incomprehensible or taboo topics. Naturally, this can also work. However, this approach requires a sophisticated marketing and communication strategy, which is much more difficult to implement. Behind a deliberately nonchalant and provocative appearance , there is a concept which is generally a much more complex than it might appear to be at first.

After we have clarified the elements of our art's substantive foundation, once we know what statements our works want to convey , and we have sought out people who would potentially be interested in our art with the help of a customer profile, the development of a communication path can take place during the third step.

5.3) Communication Path

In order to catch the fancy of those who are interested in our art, and who would be worth considering as potential buyers, we must organise our communication – that is, our contact with the customers and the manner in which we publicly present our art - in an appropriate manner. A well planned campaign which focuses our energies and resources on this group, from which interest in our art is likely to be expected. It is beneficial to combine these considerations in a concept. On the one hand, this allows resources to be managed better, and, on the other hand, it allows errors to be traced back better.

The development process of a communication strategy which reaches art buyers is composed of three parts. Step by step, we want to lead ourselves into the following individual phases with their individual objectives and their corresponding market tools in mind. The implementation and execution of the application of market tools should be adapted to the demands and the expectations of the audience profile.

The starting point of our campaign is built by the content of our art, with the aim of finding the appropriate public. In the first phase , it is a question of whether interested parties can be won over. The fancy of a wide audience – and not just of the developed target audience – should be caught. The aim is to drive as much attention to yourself as possible. This is best achieved by means of a provocation , by means of something spectacular, to multiply opinions, including the opinions of those who form opinions and who are dominant on the market (news papers, magazines, galleries, critics,...) and who could speed up the circulation of our cause and attract attention to it. First and foremost, presentation and networking are available as market tools. The most suitable provocative idea should be the art idea which is adjusted so that you can move up the market. An artist who wants to market tasteful still life would certainly draw attention to himself by doing provocative body painting on the market square, but then he would not be attracting any attention to his still life. If you succeed at arousing interest, you should be able to move up in your career with information and content. The interested parties must be provided with an opportunity to have an easier access to particular works, as well as to find the individual person of the artist. In doing so, publications by the daily press are particularly beneficial, as are publications in brochures, or in flyers, which can be used for this purpose.

At this point, it is necessary to convince these interested parties about us and about our work. To this end, you should be able to present a clear offer and an overview over your own work and its contents. Special publications and presentations, which go into things in more depth, are now meaningful, e.g. a web site which presents your working method, is an advantage. In order to decide whether or not to buy something, the interested party needs something that validates and hedges his choice. In a suitable tool market mix this can be positively influenced. Everything that points to reputation and safety is an advantage. Should you, for example, have any prominent or any personally interested parties, this can create a high level of trust. To begin with, it is advisable to give proper thought to how the conclusion of a contract with the potentially interested parties can be carried out with no difficulties, be these parties galleries and/or private buyers. The know-how market tool is particularly useful here. If, for example, you need to organise an exhibition overseas, you must know how you can ship the pictures there. Similarly, you should be familiar with how purchase agreements are construed, as it would be more than unfortunate to lose an interested party prospective shortly before the successful conclusion of the transaction due to formal inconsistencies.

Basically, it is easier to keep regular customers than it is to win new customers. You should bear this in mind after a successful transaction and act accordingly. Therefore, it is not only important to validate customers' decisions during the persuasion phase, but it is important that you also give them the feeling that they have made the right decision in the long term. With a market tool mix of publications and networks, this can be successfully achieved. Everyone who has invested in art will be happy to discover that an exhibition by an artist in whom they invested is taking place in a museum, and that they might be induced to buy replacement works.

This overall process of finding interested parties, of persuading them and of having a relationship with them is rarely straight forward. Sometimes, reorientations or intermediate targets which call for flexibility are required. The ultimate goal is achieved through strategically planned milestones, but the moments in between are anything but rigid and unalterable. Through every stage of your communication campaign, you learn about your market , your public and you even get to know yourself as a participant in the market better. New experiences and impulses significantly influence an artist's career and development on the art market. It is all the more important to implement the steps in a sensible manner, in order to avoid losing your bearings.

6) Sales talk

Traditional art sales are about culture striving, but getting to the core of art sale it is a process of personal motivation and emotions. The tough reality of the art market, which makes things tough for artists, is that people do not really buy cultural values or cultural needs for the sake of it. What people are buying, even in art, is individual desires. Art becomes a purchase only when it is engaging us on a personal level and we get really motivated for what it is doing or what it will do for us.

Understanding the art market as a process of satisfying desires breaks the art market's complexity down. Art and selling art is becoming the process of motivation. Motivation of art buying does not occur through the 45 minutes of an exhibition opening talk. It is more a instant moment like falling in love. It is one of those things in a sales presentation, a moment or two when a person suddenly makes up their mind, thus deciding that this is something they really want, something that they desperately need, that relates to a deep desire and can be justified with logic after they have made the subconscious decision.

So when its coming down to sale art, two thing are important. How to build up a tremendous want in the buyers mind for your artwork and how to be able to represent their own want in a way that they are able to justify buying with logic. Art selling becomes a process of helping someone to get motivated on a subconscious level. If you want people to have something badly enough, they usually find a way to justify it with just a little bit of help from you. The good news is that the method for this is in a way natural and simple. In terms of a formula, the primary motivating factor behind all human behavior is the desire to avoid the negative, like pain and the desire or the need for the positive, to gain pleasure, grow or thrive. Pleasure and pain are twin forces of human behavior. Understanding this pleasure and pain formula becomes the main tool of persuasion. If we want to persuade someone to do anything, we have to understand that people do things because we can tell them to do them in a way that is convenient to their agenda. Set in relation to the sale: people are doing things for reasons, so they have to associate the action of buying something the action of creating tremendous pleasure and the action of not buying to the action of not creating pain.

Success in the art market is based on the creation of those twin motivations of pleasure and pain, with integrity and elegance. During the process of art selling, we assist the buyer to get what they want by unleashing the most powerful force within them: the power to create change. This is a process of emotions and consequences. To persuade is to provide an outlook on positive consequences with (or without) using the tool of negative consequences. This technique involves a mindset in which you really bear in mind the buyers' best interest and aim to build trust. Selling art is to step over the threshold of being the producer of art and helping somebody to gain cultural values. This human side of sales is an important step in gaining buyers' sympathy and trust. The next part of the process is to help the buyer to get a clear vision of what they really want and how the art will help them to fulfill this. In doing so, they are linking in their mind what they are going to get through the value of this artwork, in terms of their desires. In exchange of money, they will get value.

The process of selling is finding out a buyer's beliefs and values. Finding out that they are linked to a process and a thing. This is mostly a reason why so many artists have problems selling their art. Firstly, their perspective on their artwork changes from their own opinion, to the more important opinion of the art buyer. Secondly, in the eyes of the buyer, the artist is becoming a salesperson. It is a sad truth that people have certain negative emotions that they associate with sales people. They link less pleasurable emotions with sales people, because of the experience they had before. An artist should never assume that the buyer understands that they are not an average salesperson, but that they are an artist representing his or her art. It takes a conscious effort to change what people associate things with in order to change their behavior.

If a person does not buy something, they associate more pain or negative outcomes with buying something than they do with not buying it. And if a person does buy something, it is because they associate much more pleasure to doing so than they do to not doing so. We can us this to provide a situation in which buying means pleasure and not pain. This formula is simple, yet powerful.

Finding and understanding people's lack of fulfillment or pain and making that absence or disturbance obvious to them is the most important part of art selling. Guiding a person and making them feel the cultural or personal gap before healing it through a new cultural experience in the form of the art work, is the main mission during the art sales talk. In this way, selling art becomes a "hurt and healing" process to generate emotional reasons and guiding the buyer to a solution so they can justify the purchase with logic.

The core of this process in art sales is based on emotional aspects. The person who is interested or the art lover, is doing things for emotional reasons, not for logical reasons. With a good understanding of what the buyer is lacking, and by showing them what they are missing, as well as their hurt or pain, the buyer is motivated to change. Assuming that they trust us, he or she will tell us how art can fulfill the inner gap, heal their wound or give them what they are missing on their own.

The empathic art sale is a 3 steps process:

1. Listen, find and understand their interest and what they want and are not getting (everybody wants something.)
2. Make their gap obvious, so that it disturbs them.
3. Motivate and solve the problem by using their reasons and the benefits of your art.

Linking somebody's desires to culture consists in linking our art to their desires. Artists must make buyers realize what feelings they desire and want the most, and render them compelling and very real for them. The aspect of associating not buying with pain can be helpful when it

comes to making a decision, but it must
not be a part of our strategy. To get to this
point of implementing this process, artists
must build up an understanding of their
point of view. In other words, selling a
product with massive cultural and
personal value must mean a win-win
situation. To do this, we have to find
emotional reasons for the buyer, including
interests, desires and the pain that they
are feeling. It is important to make this
person aware of their pain and of what
they are missing; to stir up emotions that
are based on their own desires and needs.
Mastering the emotional side of selling is
mostly natural and easy, that's why it's
important to keep an eye on adding logic
as well. It is about giving the buyer the
needed information to justify their reasons
for buying.

Most of that process is an empathic
interaction. But buying needs emotional
reasons and justifications of logic. Our
mission is to feed this logical reason, but
more importantly, to dig for that
implementing emotion, to find it, make it
obvious and likeable for them, conform it
as important and when necessary disturb
it. Art selling is a mastery of empathy and
understanding people's needs and how to
guide them. It's not a mystery skill, all we
need is the ability to listen and an elegant
way to ask questions. Questions are the

main key to understanding and guiding buyers. With questions, we are not only gaining important knowledge, but we are controlling focus and, consequently, the direction that a conversation is taking. A question is something that our mind cannot avoid reacting to and forming an opinion on before producing feelings on how we relate or do not relate to the content of the question. It is up to artists to choose on what the buyer will focus and how they will feel during the process.

Beside the questions there are more tools to navigate the buyer though the fulfillment of his desires. It is important to set some primary facts in our own mind before we even start the conversation with our art buying person.
When we think of our sale as a line from point A (the buyer is interested in a art work) to a point B (the buyer is handing over the money) we can imagine this as a straight line between those points. Of course this won't be a straight line. Sometimes, the situation, new events or an unpredictable reaction of the buyer will make a twist in our line. Because of this, we have to decide first, what are the limits of our sales process are. How much are we are willing to leave the path for irrelevant arguments, or arguments about reducing the price, and other things that are just consuming our time and energy. This

depends on our willingness and on the fun that we are connecting with art selling. These borders make it easy to lead the conversation like during a waltz dance. If you do not control the situation in the beginning of the sale you will never be able to control the situation in the end. Like a professional dancer, a good sales person does not wait and see, he or she is leading back to the center of the dance floor. It's to both benefits to stay focused on what is necessary according to the buyers' real desires and lead them softly to the right decision.

It is only impossible to stay on this line or get commitment in a conversation in which the buyer has the feeling that we are not 100% addicted and aware of them. The buyer is committed to the artist just as much as the artist is committed to him. Commitments are the basis of influence. They start with an interest in an art work, but, once the buyer makes a commitment, they begin to feel pressure to be consistent with the commitments they have made. If we are consistent, then we become most likely trusted. If we can get an art buyer to say yes to the things that are connecting his desires with art work and its benefits, it is going to be really hard for him or her to back off in the end.
If this building of commitments is happening in positive and enthusiastic

surroundings, in which we are giving the buyer the feeling of understanding his desires without any pressure, it becomes a positive experience for them. Our positive approach and enthusiasm has the power to transform. Positive enthusiasm is like a gravitation field for a positive outcome. In a longer conversation, a constant, enthusiastic, positive emotion is transferred to the buyer. It is important to understand the conversation as uplifting someone's feeling to the same level of enthusiasm for the art work that artists already have.

This feeling of positive care is also what transforms the conversation into a closer relationship. We have given enormous value to this person in the conversation and, in showing how much this art work is worth, we are really fulfilling their needs. This builds value for him or her. It is easy to exchange this value with the buyer, who is already inquiring about the amount of money it is costing. If we really care and can show that we are giving them the significant value that is written on the price tag, it's not a problem to ask for the money. The sales point in the conversation is not such a mystery. It is worth to remember that we sometimes have the wrong perspective and in reality the person is willing to buy, so it is always important to AFM, ask for the money. It is a game of balance between getting into the persons wants, without losing ourselves in unsolvable obstacles and guiding the person softly to fulfilling their desires by buying our art.

The best think about selling art is that there is no such thing as a negative outcome. The person who did not buy participated in a cultural experience that will guide them back to art. If we worked well, they may even come back to us. And we found out more about our art though a perspective that we couldn't understand and serve at the moment, but that will expand our understanding of our work. There are many tools that can help you on the way. The quickest way to find the "soft spot" is to ask questions about the person's deep needs or deep desires is building rapport. This means that they respond to us.

Questions provide us with a lot of things. They provide us with the opportunity to find out what's really going on in this person's mind. Get to know them and find out what their real motivations and beliefs are. When we know what the person's beliefs are, it is easy to spot the one that we can align with and assure that we are building in congruency with those beliefs. With questions, we are also able to test the situation without pushing or breaking the rapport, even to do things like do test closes of the sale. The benefit of questions also takes pressure off you. It gives the buyer the possibility to contribute content to the conversation, so we do not have to carry all of the pressure of entertaining and presentation. We are building something that has been developed together, and people support what they are creating.

Like rapport starting from a common point of culture, our congruency is keeping us in the role of an artist. As an artist, it is beneficial to keep matching what we are painting with what people experience – that is, the things that we express, in a verbal and non verbal way. It is important to remember that if a person feels most certain it comes from a transparent emotion. People need to feel certain when they make the decision to buy, that they are getting more pleasure and less pain. Only in this trusting environment of the conversation can we begin to anchor the positive feelings towards the pleasure of buying. In a way, selling is nothing more than connecting the positive with our goal or outcome. If we can get a person in an intense feeling or state and we are consistently connecting this positive experience with a different occurrence, we are linking this feeling or state with this occurrence or anchor. This is making it possible in the future that they will go back to that state just by using the anchor again. It's the most efficient way to put a person back into a positive state that will help them to focus on his or their desires. All we are doing during the sale is making a positive connection and interrupting a negative vision that cannot be reasoned with any more. Sometimes people get in a state of mind or emotion where they get stuck. It is important to understand that it is useless to fight this focusing or emotional development, it's not working because it is feeding on contrast and that's what they expect you to do. As long as they are in a state in which they are connecting negativity or pain to the art work, they are not going to buy it. We can interrupt the pattern of focusing on negative. Depending on the person and on the connection level, we can do or ask something that is totally unexpected.

It is important to keep a perspective in the conversation that is detached from instant action and reaction of feelings. From such a perspective, it is easy to change the reception of subjects, use contrast, interrupt patterns or build on commitments. How we often feel about anything comes back to our perspective or frame on which we are looking. The way in which we decide to connect a feeling with a meaning is, for us, a manner of framing things. To persuade them, we must understand the principle of framing. We can use different approaches to give the buyer a different perspective and to open up a door for them out of the state that they had got themselves into. The easiest way is to stop a person building up or running into an objection is by creating a point of view that is different from their original one. For example: If a person is really in love with a painting and the room might be too small for it, we can change the meaning into an explanation that, from now on, the will live inside of the picture. Often try to be playful by changing perspectives. Handle objections before they become totally firm.

When the art buyer gets used to seeing something from a certain point of view, it is hard to change their point of view. Buyers also tend to defend their perspective once they have decided upon it. If you want to overcome these objections, change the buyer's focus by getting them to focus on a new question or on a new way of looking at things. Sometimes it is wise to change or postpone the whole discussion for a while.

In most cases, when the buyer is not entirely certain that this objection is a firm one, we can transform that objection into a question. This helps them to focus again, or to evaluate the situation in a new light. In practice ,this happens frequently during the price discussion. A remark about art being too expensive can easily be turned into a question about compared to what the art is too expensive.

Art selling can be an art form for artists. The pure technique is useless unless you develop a joy in spending your time eye to eye with art loving and buying people. Empathy is a useful key. It is all about listening to your customer, which should be 80 % of the conversation, 20 % is us talking, but not about ourselves; about guiding this person into our art with their own point of view and feelings. All it takes in the beginning is effort to become an "ear and heart person" and to focus on somebody's wants and point of view. It is an open secret that it is easier to sell to a person who really desires a picture for 1000€, than it is to sell to a person who has just a want to buy art at 100€. So, art selling often comes down to your ability to change your state. State management requires us to control our own emotions, ego and become a more empathic person.

The first step

Selling art can become a practice for personal growth and motivation for art. Motivation is not something that we have; it is something that we generate. Pay awareness to yourself and notice what are the things that naturally pushing you to successes. Perhaps it was curiosity, frustration, the duty you feel to make your creativity prosper, or maybe it was something entirely different. Come up with a list of what motivates you. You can fall back on this list if you have a fall back in your art career. And don't worry even when you have a fall back or decide to take a break: the idea to exchange your art for wealth will not let you go and get you.. Just take your time. Even if you do not have the time, then just break this book down into chewable slices. Think of your art career like you do of your art work; in your art, it is necessary to take time to prepare your materials and ideas. The same goes for your art career. So, please take the time for your art career to develop in an organic manner. Think about it this way: money is one of the easiest tools to buy you time for your art. This book is reducing the amount of time that you waste, so you can take time to practice and master your skills for the art market, and to develop your career step by step. Learning and mastering your skills is the part of your career that will pay off later. The toughest obstacle we will have to face during our art career is our mindset. Having a point of view that life is a learning and growing process that cannot occur in a comfort zone is an advantage. Of course, the life path of an artist isn't easy, things are not just going to happen. Going down the path of a financially successful artist is the most desired career path and field of human development possible: IT IS THE ART. When things are happening, the meaning that we give to those events is critical: will it be the end because our first endeavor was a failure, or was our first endeavor a possibility to learn, to try a different approach and to give our wisdom to others once we got farther down the line so that they can overcome the same problem much more quickly?

My hope was to pack in this lean free version as much helpful content for you as I can, but in this version I cannot answer every question. Take the effort in adopting the knowledge to your situation. If you need more help I have put a lot of effort in larger version of this book with questioners and a included career planer that will guide you in a more specific way. Every artist's individuality, starting position and art market has different variables. This was also the reason why I almost kept this knowhow exclusively for coaching and teaching one on one. But this individuality of artists is what gave me the courage to boil everything down to these pages. As an artist, you can use your creative power to adapt the guidelines and to be curious enough to find a way through challenges. The challenges that are not subject to this literature are also the ones that are making your art unique. It is necessary to overcome them, because they provide you with the experience that is necessary so that you never face those challenges again. One message that is important for me, is that you do not have to be blessed with anything special to make a living from art, nor do you have to have anything really extraordinary to achieve this. Once it is happening to you, you are going into the mindset; "Yes, of course it is natural, it is the next step I had to take". For me a change of the mind set started with my exhibitions in NY. Once you overcome the threshold of earning the necessities of your living, every big sum of money is just something that ends up in the next bigger art project. If you have already a mindset that lets you enjoy a free coffee, because a waitress liked your drawing on a napkin and gave you a free cup, you will also in enjoy bigger payments. Being aware of this and enjoying the privilege of selling art is something that will always keep you on track. The feeling of gratitude is significant, it was a privilege for me to sell a painting a few weeks ago. It made possible for me to spend 5 weeks travelling through India for inspiration. But it is wise to remind oneself that this is happening because of my art and for my art. In short, possessing the right mindset for the art market is a dare. The best way is to focus on the joy of creativity. For me, it is equally enjoyable to receive a large sum of money thanks to an art deal BUT in the same manner, I am enjoying your contribution of time reading this, because someone is honoring my effort and creativity.

The art market offers many rewards. It is wise to start enjoying and appreciating what we earn with every step on the way.

Your art is worth it, go for it!

Many artists who "made it" in the market and I envy you in a way, all of the adventures for the sake of your art are yet to come. Perhaps you can hear this voice inside you, telling you that just producing art is not enough, that sharing your art will be a benefit for you and that there are people out there who are waiting for your artwork right now, without knowing that you or your artwork even exists. This is also what was motivating me to get out there and seek the ones who would appreciate my message and my creativity after I finished my art studies. I wish I could skip some of the experience, like when I had to run from one gallery to the next, only to find out that it was not the right approach. But in a way, even this frustration now symbolizes the golden energetic time of my first steps. Even those cold foggy streets of London that I walked down, with my artwork under my arm, have a sort Dickens-like glamour now, that I wouldn't have missed.

Art can always surprise one. If there is one thing that is worth all of your efforts, that is art. The only thing it needs is the decision to make the first step. You have already achieved this by reading this book. It is not my wish to put pressure on you. Maybe you will put it away or just try it for a few days. It doesn't matter, because, from now on, there will be this voice in the back of your head, telling you that it is possible and an adventure is waiting for you. Maybe one day an opportunity will just appear out of nowhere and you will be prepared because of this book. Maybe one day it will occur to you that your creativity is a unique, blessed gift and that it is worth opening a new chapter in your career as an upcoming artist. I think that there is no motivation needed for artists to take his or hers first step. His or her creativity will find a way at some point, and, eventually, their art will blossom. My hope is that the contribution of this book will make your journey more comfortable, enjoyable and with fewer danger d-tours, and that, some day, we will meet in the wide ocean that is commonly referred to as the art market.

Epilog

how to kill creativity - the perfection bullet.

It's easy to say "You just don't understand, I am a perfectionist." is the perfectionist's lie, that crafty and vain and elegant delay logic shared with a high-chin. It's far to easy to tangled up in doubt or distraction, and so we have yet to commit the grueling focus, toil, sweat, and investment that real work and creativity requires. The reason most of us have not finished is because we have yet to truly begin. In a way perhaps we fear ourselves. If there is such a thing as a "perfectionist," we should at least be precise and call it like it is: "I am scared and distracted, and so I have yet to proceed or complete." If there is perfection it would be wise, to know that the act of "perfecting" something comes only after completing and releasing it. If such a thing exists, it's only happens after the terrible mess of creativity has been waded through with heart and discipline. If there is real magic it happens after a thing is done as best as possible given the time constraints and after it can finally be shared with the world and beaten up and commented on and criticized and iterated, than we would know that day dreaming is not enough. Perhaps we could learn that it's only begins once you see our work and art in the hands of others, once we see their eyes shine with joy or squint with repelling. But how to become the artist, the master? With action, not perpetual analysis, moving us toward a more perfected state; that initiative alone propels us to real glory and greatness. Sensing that true high standards demand implementation not anxious apathy; that flawlessness is a fiction of the dreamer and has no use in the reality of the learner.

But how to actually completed the thing, overcome fear and distraction, living the comfort zone behind and actually allow days and weeks and months of courage and commitment, allow all the sloppiness and the feedback, allow the grand challenge to ego, allow the highs and lows of inspired and meaningful striving? By realizing that it wasn't perfection we were after at all, but rather creating and contributing something great and worthwhile. Following the call of duty and discipline to finishing the things we dream of, we become alive and whole and handing over our art to those we serve, no matter how imperfect, keeping our focus to fulfill our mission.

Let's not kill creativity with perfection, let us lose the perfectionist's lie and get at it. Let's get on the path of masters, not perfectionists, no matter how stony the first steps are. Working hard and take thrill in the toil and hardship and meaning that inspired action gives us. Just create and share and learn and reinvent with joy and complete it and release it and love it and allow our works to live under the sun for some growing, beautifying and let our creativity thrive.

Heinrich Denke